APRIL REIMER

PRAY
FOR
CANADA

— A PRAYER JOURNAL —

PRAY FOR CANADA
Copyright © 2025 by April Reimer
Author photo credit: Cynthia Korman

All rights reserved. Neither this publication nor any part of this publication may be reproduced or transmitted in any form or by any means, electronic or mechanical, including photocopying, recording or any information storage and retrieval system, without permission in writing from the author.

Scripture quotations marked (NLT) are taken from the Holy Bible, New Living Translation, copyright ©1996, 2004, 2015 by Tyndale House Foundation. Used by permission of Tyndale House Publishers, Carol Stream, Illinois 60188. All rights reserved. Scripture quotations marked (NIV) are taken from the Holy Bible, New International Version®, NIV®. Copyright © 1973, 1978, 1984, 2011 by Biblica, Inc.™ Used by permission of Zondervan. All rights reserved worldwide. www.zondervan.com The "NIV" and "New International Version" are trademarks registered in the United States Patent and Trademark Office by Biblica, Inc.™

ISBN: 978-1-4866-2661-8
eBook ISBN: 978-1-4866-2662-5

Word Alive Press
119 De Baets Street Winnipeg, MB R2J 3R9
www.wordalivepress.ca

Cataloguing in Publication information can be obtained from Library and Archives Canada.

For Jesus.
Thank You for carrying me.

Introduction

Would you like to join me on an adventure? I'm going to start to pray for our country. Over the last few months, every time I hear the national anthem—and specifically our request for the Lord to keep our land glorious and free—it's been striking me that I need to pray.

The Lord has blessed us so much in this country, but I'm afraid our culture is shifting quickly. With all my heart, I'm asking the Lord to bring fresh fire to His Church in this country so we will see Him do great things!

This journal is a small guide to help focus our prayers. Feel free to use it however works best for you. If you feel the need to pray for a certain area more than one day in a row, do it! If you want to complete the journal once and then go back and do it again, please do!

There is space to record your prayers. Just remember that this is *your* space. If you want to write out your prayers word for word, you can do that. You could include point-form notes, or even draw in that space if that's how you enjoy praying. Feel free to get as creative with this as you want.

You will notice there is also space to record any answers you receive. If you wouldn't mind, when you see answers to your prayers, could you send me a note about that? My email address is aprilshope24@gmail.com. Hopefully at some point I'll be able to share those answers in some format. Big or small answers are all important!

Let's seek the Lord together and pray for our country.

1

PRAYERS FOR CANADA

"God, keep our land glorious and free…"

O LORD, God of heaven, the great and awesome God who keeps his covenant of unfailing love with those who love him and obey his commands, listen to my prayer! Look down and see me praying night and day for your people Israel. I confess that we have sinned against you. Yes, even my own family and I have sinned! We have sinned terribly by not obeying the commands, decrees, and regulations that you gave us through your servant Moses.

Please remember what you told your servant Moses: "If you are unfaithful to me, I will scatter you among the nations. But if you return to me and obey my commands and live by them, then even if you are exiled to the ends of the earth, I will bring you back to the place I have chosen for my name to be honored."

The people you rescued by your great power and strong hand are your servants. O Lord, please hear my prayer! Listen to the prayers of those of us who delight in honoring you. Please grant me success today by making the king favorable to me. Put it into his heart to be kind to me. (Nehemiah 1:5–11, NLT)

PRAY FOR CANADA

> **LET'S START HERE:**
> - *Pray for the Holy Spirit to move across our country.*
> - *Pray for federal, provincial, and territorial governments.*
> - *Pray for boldness for the church, that the Gospel will be shared without fear.*
> - *Pray for many Canadians to hear the Gospel and be saved.*
> - *Pray that the Lord will give the Church love for Him and for each other.*
> - *Pray for your local church and pastor.*
> - *Pray for Christians throughout Canada.*
> - *Pray that the Lord will raise up strong pastors to lead His Church through this season.*
> - *Pray for a fresh love of God's Word to flood churches across the country.*
> - *Pray for the children and youth of this country to be hungry for God and search for Him until they find Him.*
> - *Pray that God will be glorified as we pray for our country.*

Be always on the watch, and pray that you may be able to escape all that is about to happen, and that you may be able to stand before the Son of Man. (Luke 21:36, NIV)

SCRIPTURE READING: MATTHEW 6:5–13

"Lord, teach us to pray…" (Luke 11:1, NIV) We don't know what kind of day it was when the disciples said this. Cloudy? Sunny? Too hot? Cool breeze? But we do know that the disciples of Jesus asked Him to teach them to pray.

With everything Scripture tells us they saw, it's no wonder they wanted to pray like Jesus did. When Jesus prayed, miracles happened.

Has there ever been a time when you prayed and that prayer was answered so dramatically that you knew it could only have been Jesus? Or have you never really seen a prayer answered that you can remember?

I was once asked how many times a day Christians

PRAYERS FOR CANADA

are required to pray. Do we know what distinguishes our prayer lives from those of people in other religions? We don't have to pray a set number of occasions per day. We don't have to pray at certain times. We can pray anytime, anywhere. We are so privileged as Christians that we can have an open, ongoing conversation with our Savior. He even taught us how to pray.

The most beautiful thing about the Lord's prayer is that it binds us across denominational lines. We can pray this prayer together and watch the Lord answer it in our own lives. Today, if you're struggling to know exactly how or what to pray, start with the Lord's prayer.

Reassuringly, Jesus tells us in Matthew 6:8 that *"your Father knows what you need before you ask him"* (NIV). It's such a relief to know that the Lord already knows what we need! I don't know how this makes you feel, but it gives me courage to pray.

What part of the Lord's prayer resonates with you the most? Write that verse below.

Answered Prayers

PRAY FOR CANADA

JOURNAL

PRAYERS FOR CANADA

JOURNAL

2
Prince Edward Island

Home of Anne of Green Gables

Industries include agriculture, fisheries, tourism, bioscience, and advanced manufacturing.[1]

Pray for Christians in PEI:
- That they will follow Jesus faithfully.
- That they will share their faith boldly
- That they will revive His Church there.

Fun Facts
- PEI has its own provincial tartan.
- This province is the so-called "cradle of confederation." The founding fathers met in Charlottetown in 1864 to unify the provinces that would form Canada.
- It's Canada's only island province.
- PEI is also known as the golf capital of Canada.[2]

FIND two churches on the Island, send emails, and ask how you can pray for them. Remember that churches can be in both small towns and cities. List the two churches below:

1.
2.

PRAY FOR CANADA

SCRIPTURE READING: PSALM 32

David wrote this psalm, and it is such a powerful one! He opens with a statement on forgiveness. David would have been in a unique position because he knew what it was like to have sins that needed to be forgiven. I wonder if he thought about what that forgiveness felt like as he wrote this psalm.

He guides the reader through what it felt like to have sin, and then what it felt like to be forgiven. Then in Psalm 32:6, he encourages the faithful to pray to the Lord while He may be found. The promise included with this verse is beautiful; the rising of the waters will not reach the faithful.

Repentance is a unique gift to us. The Lord has made a way for us to be cleansed from our sin. If we are left on our own, we will wander off the path the Lord has for us.

> **CHECK THE NEWS ABOUT PEI.**
> *How can you pray for PEI today?*

Sometimes I have been guilty of seeing repentance as something bad, when in reality it is the best part of prayer. Knowing that I have confessed my sins and been forgiven leads me to a stronger relationship with the Lord.

Read 1 John 1:9, then take a few moments today to confess any sins you haven't prayed about yet. Just imagine what the Lord will do with a repentant Church! So often we want revival, but we fail to remember that revival needs to start in our own hearts; repentance is the start of revival.

DAY 2: PRINCE EDWARD ISLAND

What do you think it means that we should pray to the Lord while He may be found? Write your answer in the space below.

ANSWERED PRAYERS

PRAY FOR CANADA

JOURNAL

DAY 2: PRINCE EDWARD ISLAND

Journal

3

Nova Scotia

Peggy's Cove and the Cabot Trail

The Bluenose schooner, a racing ship, sailed from Nova Scotia and is so famous that it made the back of the Canadian dime.[3]

Pray for Christians in Nova Scotia:

- To overflow with love for each other and their communities.
- To see church growth.
- To crave Bible reading.

Scripture Reading: Daniel 9:1-23

What would happen if we had Christian leaders who took the time to pray for our country? Daniel was one man who held a secular job in Babylon, but he also knew the power of prayer. In today's reading, we can see that not only did he pray earnestly for his people, but he also received an answer!

Those of us who hold secular jobs have probably been encouraged to separate our faith from our jobs. We can see that Daniel did not follow this practice. He did his job well, but he still held the Lord in the highest esteem and relied on God for help.

PRAY FOR CANADA

In the earlier chapters of Daniel, when did he place his faith above his job? Take a look back through the chapters and write your answer below.

WHAT NEWS STORIES ARE CURRENTLY HAPPENING IN NOVA SCOTIA?
How can you pray for this province?

Find two churches to contact and pray for. Record them below:

1.

2.

DAY 3: NOVA SCOTIA

We may not have leaders who pray for our country, but that doesn't mean we should not pray! As the Church, we are called to be salt and light. The most effective way to do that is to spend regular time with the Lord in prayer and reading His Word.

How will you find time to regularly pray in your schedule? Prayers don't have to be limited to the country in general. There are many things you can put on your list!

Below, write out a plan for when exactly you will pray this week. For example, how many times will you schedule prayer? How long will you pray? What time of day, or days of the week, will you pray?

Answered Prayers

PRAY FOR CANADA

JOURNAL

DAY 3: NOVA SCOTIA

JOURNAL

4

NEW BRUNSWICK
Province of Lighthouses

PRAY FOR CHRISTIANS IN NOVA SCOTIA:
- To share their faith.
- To obey God's call.
- To overflow with joy.

FUN FACTS
- The St. John River flows backwards twice a day, every day, thanks to the tides in the Bay of Fundy.
- Snowblowers were invented in New Brunswick.
- Moncton has a neat spot named Magnetic Hill, where things roll uphill. Yes, apparently if you put your car in neutral, it will roll up this hill!
- New Brunswick's provincial tree is the balsam fir.
- There are at least forty-eight lighthouses in New Brunswick.
- Beaver Harbour was the first community in British North America to forbid slavery.[4]

SCRIPTURE READING: LUKE 18:1–8
Wanting to reinforce to His disciples that they needed to pray and not give up, Jesus told them the parable in this passage.

PRAY FOR CANADA

Do you ever feel like you need justice? The Lord will ensure that we get true justice. He can hear us calling out to Him through the day and night. Notice that this promise is directed at His *"chosen ones"* (Luke 18:7). Christians have full access to this promise, but nonbelievers do not have the same promise.

Was there ever a time in your life when you needed justice and the Lord answered? Or has there been a time when you called on the Lord day and night to get an answer to prayer, and it finally came?

If you have never experienced an answered prayer after praying faithfully for weeks, months, or possibly years, do not stop praying! The Lord will answer.

The last verse in this passage is quite powerful. In the first part of the verse, Jesus promises that God will see that His

> ### What's in the News?
> *How can you pray for New Brunswick?*

> *Find two churches online. Contact them to see how you can pray for them. If you don't get a response, check their church bulletin online and see how you can pray.*
>
> 1.
>
> 2.

DAY 4: NEW BRUNSWICK

children get justice. Then He asks a stunning question: when He returns, will He find faith on the earth?

Do you ever wonder whether there will be any faith left by the time Jesus returns? Look up verses related to faith to discover what the Scriptures tell us about this important topic. Write the references in the space provided, or write a few verses out by hand.

And remember that *"he who began a good work in you will carry it on to completion until the day of Jesus Christ"* (Philippians 1:6, NIV).

Answered Prayers

Journal

DAY 4: NEW BRUNSWICK

JOURNAL

5

Newfoundland and Labrador

Canada's Tourist Province

Industry here includes oil and gas, mining, fisheries, and hydroelectricity.[5]

Pray for Christians in Newfoundland and Labrador:
- To be filled with peace.
- To pray with the sick and lonely.
- To call the Church back to the Lord

Fun Facts:
- Newfoundland has North America's easternmost point.
- Newfoundland is one of the world's largest islands.
- Ferries are available to take you to the nearby French islands of Saint Pierre and Miquelon.
- The island has its own time zone.[6]

Scripture Reading: John 17:20–26
When the Passover meal was served, Jesus and the disciples would have been together in the upper room. This year's Passover might

PRAY FOR CANADA

> ### How We Can Pray:
> *Email two churches and get their prayer requests:*
>
> 1.
>
> 2.

> ### Check the news.
> *Check the news. Is there anything specific to pray for in Newfoundland and Labrador?*

have seemed routine, but it was different than every other year. This is the year Jesus was to be crucified and then resurrected, becoming the Passover Lamb.

In the final few minutes of peace in that room with His disciples, before they left for the Mount of Olives where Jesus would be betrayed and arrested, Jesus prayed.

John, being the youngest disciple and one who sat closest to Jesus at the table that night, recorded this prayer for us.

Does it surprise you that Jesus prayed for you? In those final moments of the prayer, did He look into the future to see those who would come to faith through the ages? This shows us that Jesus is not distant. We were on His mind before He went to the cross.

Look up Hebrews 2:17–18. What does this passage tell us about Jesus making atonement for our sins? What role does He have now? Thank You, Lord, for not being distant from us!

DAY 5: NEWFOUNDLAND AND LABRADOR

Write out the verse in today's passage that leaves the biggest impression on you.

Answered Prayers

PRAY FOR CANADA

JOURNAL

DAY 5: NEWFOUNDLAND AND LABRADOR

JOURNAL

6
Quebec
A Bit of French-Speaking Europe in Canada

Pray for Christians in Quebec:
- To share Jesus with their communities.
- To create Christian resources in French.
- To see a revival across Quebec.

In June 2019, Quebec passed Bill 21, a bill that bans public servants from wearing religious symbols while they are at work in June 2019. This confirmed the province's secular status.[7]

Did you know that Protestant Christians make up only two percent of the population in Quebec in the 2021 census?[8]

PRAY FOR CANADA

SCRIPTURE READING: PSALM 102:17

Do you ever wonder whether it makes a difference if a wealthy person prays instead of a poor person? Does it seem as though the Lord will look after the rich more closely than He looks after the poor? Today's verse portrays a beautiful picture of how the Lord responds to prayers. Write it out below.

Throughout the Bible, we can see that the Lord takes special care of the poor. Do any examples of this come to mind? Scripture also contains references to barriers being broken when we are baptized into Christ (Galatians 3:26–28).

Today, whether you have lots of earthly possessions or few, pray while knowing that the Lord hears and answers your prayers!

WHAT NEWS STORIES CAN YOU FIND ABOUT QUEBEC?
How can you pray for this province?

Contact two churches in Quebec. How can you pray for these churches?

1.

2.

DAY 6: QUEBEC

ANSWERED PRAYERS

PRAY FOR CANADA

Journal

Day 6: Quebec

Journal

7

ONTARIO

Niagara Falls, Toronto Blue Jays, Great Lakes

Pray for Christians in Ontario:
- To stand on the truth of God's Word.
- To trust God and follow where He leads.
- To be gentle with each other and the unsaved.

Fun Facts:
- Amethyst is the official mineral of Ontario.
- Ontario had its own World War II spy school in Whitby.
- Ontario has some of the world's most dangerous rapids.[9]

Scripture Reading: Ephesians 1:18–23

No one could pen a prayer quite like the apostle Paul could. This prayer stretches over a verse and a half, after which Paul adds some clarification about the power we as believers have access to.

Paul prays for the believers in Ephesus to know hope, the riches of God's glorious inheritance, and His incomparably great power. We have access to this same hope, glorious inheritance, and incomparably great power today.

PRAY FOR CANADA

I often wonder, would we pray "bigger" if we truly believed the Lord heard our prayers? Would we trust the Lord to answer our prayers beyond what we can imagine?

Pray for the Province:

What stories are in the news? How can you pray for the people of Ontario?

Pray for the Church:

List two churches below that you can pray for. If you contact them and don't receive a response, do they have bulletins listed on their websites that would indicate how you can pray for them?

1.

2.

DAY 7: ONTARIO

In the space provided below, write out the part of this passage that speaks directly to you. What do you learn through Paul's prayer?

ANSWERED PRAYERS

PRAY FOR CANADA

JOURNAL

DAY 7: ONTARIO

Journal

8

Manitoba

Wheat Fields and Polar Bears

Pray for Christians in Manitoba:
- To meet together to pray.
- To grow in goodness
- To stand firm in the faith.

Manitoba's Prayer

"O Eternal and Almighty God, from whom all power and wisdom come, we are assembled here before Thee to frame such laws as may tend to the welfare and prosperity of our province.

Grant O merciful God we pray Thee, that we may desire only that which is in accordance with Thy will, that we may seek it with wisdom and know it with certainty and accomplish it perfectly.

For the glory and honour of Thy name and for the welfare of all our people. Amen."[10]

Did you know that this prayer is currently prayed before the opening of the Manitoba legislature? There may soon be some changes made to this tradition.

PRAY FOR CANADA

SCRIPTURE READING: EPHESIANS 3:14–21

This passage provides us with another prayer Paul shares for the Ephesian church. Read this passage and then write it out in the space below.

Is there a verse that stands out to you in this passage? If so, which one and why does it strike you?

What amazes me in this passage is Ephesians 3:20, where Paul writes that God can do *"immeasurably more than all we ask or imagine, according to his power that is at work within us"* (NIV). This changes the way I want to pray.

What is the biggest thing you can imagine to ask God to do for our country? Pray and ask for it, then look for the Lord to do more than what you asked for. We serve a faithful God who will answer our prayers!

STORIES IN THE NEWS TO PRAY FOR:	CHURCHES TO PRAY FOR:
	1.
	2.

DAY 8: MANITOBA

Record your thoughts below on how big you would like to see the Lord move!

Answered Prayers

PRAY FOR CANADA

JOURNAL

DAY 8: MANITOBA

JOURNAL

9

NUNAVUT

The Newest Territory

DID YOU KNOW:

- Nunavut has the longest coastline in Canada (due to all of the islands in the territory).
- Nunavut has four official languages!
- There are no roads to Nunavut – it's only accessible by sea or air.[11]

SCRIPTURE READING: COLOSSIANS 4:3–4

What would it feel like to be arrested and put in chains for the Gospel? Kept in a prison cell where it's cold, with the possibility of little or no food? Even in these circumstances, Paul did not ask the people to pray for his comfort. He didn't demand that they do more to get him out of prison. What did he ask them to pray for instead?

We have had lots of freedom to worship Jesus in Canada, so the concept of being in jail as a Christian is foreign to us. Do you think this will remain true, or can you see this changing at some point in the future? The best time to plan for such possibilities is now, before it happens. That way, we can be solid in our faith and serve the Lord in whatever circumstances He puts us.

PRAY FOR CANADA

Let's pray for the Lord to open doors in Canada for the Gospel. What He opens, no one can shut—and what He shuts, no one can open (Revelation 3:8).

> **SEE WHAT IS HAPPENING IN THE NEWS WITH NUNAVUT:**
> *How can you pray for the territory?*

> **PRAYER TIME:**
> *Which two churches can you pray for in Nunavut? How can you pray for them?*
>
> 1.
>
> 2.

DAY 9: NUNAVUT

How can we strengthen our faith in these times of freedom so we are ready if a battle comes? Write out your battle plan for strengthening your faith below. Make sure that the goals you list are attainable!

ANSWERED PRAYERS

JOURNAL

DAY 9: NUNAVUT

Journal

10

SASKATCHEWAN

Land of the Living Skies

PRAY FOR CHRISTIANS IN SASKATCHEWAN:
- To shine God's light in a darkening world.
- To encourage one another to follow God wholeheartedly.
- To endure in their faith with joy.

FUN FACTS
- Sylvite (potash) is Saskatchewan's official mineral.
- Saskatchewan has its own tartan.
- Curling is Saskatchewan's official sport.[12]

SCRIPTURE READING: 2 THESSALONIANS 1:11–12

Do you ever feel like you have to strive really hard to accomplish things for the Lord? To keep your spiritual life on track? Does it sometimes take more energy than you have?

These two verses pain such a beautiful picture of how our spiritual lives can grow. Paul, Silas, and Timothy didn't tell the Thessalonian church, "Try harder! Keep pushing through!" Instead they told the church members to keep on praying for the church. They asked God to enable them to live worthy of God's call. Then they asked the Lord to give the church power to accomplish whatever their faith prompted them to do.

PRAY FOR CANADA

Of course the Thessalonians themselves had to take action. However, they were not expected to complete these tasks in their own power.

Check the News:
How can you pray for Saskatchewan?

Find Two Churches to Pray for:

1.

2.

Day 10: Saskatchewan

How has the Lord carried you through difficult circumstances? How has He grown your faith and trust in Him? Write an example or two below.

Answered Prayers

PRAY FOR CANADA

Journal

Day 10: Saskatchewan

Journal

11
Northwest Territories

Land of the Midnight Sun and Canada's Diamond Territory!

Pray for Christians in the Northwest Territories:
- To find others to meet and pray with.
- To be filled with joy.
- To share their faith in their daily lives.

The Northwest Territories has:
- Eleven official languages!
- The Dehcho region, which is home to nineteen hot springs. Some of these can heat up to more than thirty degrees Celsius!
- The Thomsen River, which is the farthest north navigable river on the planet.
- A population of forty-four thousand.[13]

Scripture Reading: James 5:13–18
In this passage, when does James tell us to pray? Isn't it interesting that there are many situations in life when we should be praying?

PRAY FOR CANADA

Life can be difficult, even on a good day. What is your first reaction to hardship? I'm usually the type to try to fix problems on my own, but that doesn't always go so well. Often prayer seems to be my last resort instead of the first thing I do.

I'm learning that if I add prayer time to my daily schedule, the burdens of the daily grind seem to get a bit lighter, and often solutions pop up that I would never have thought of myself! When I think I'm too busy and don't have time to pray,

---

CHECK THE NEWS:
How can you pray for the NWT?

FIND TWO CHURCHES TO PRAY FOR:
See if you can contact them for ways to pray, or check their church bulletins if available:

1.

2.

DAY 11: NORTHWEST TERRITORIES

I end up running into trouble.

The last two verses in this passage talk about Elijah. Read 1 Kings 17:1–9. What details do you notice about Elijah in the first verse? How did the Lord provide for Elijah when there was no rain? Does this encourage you to pray more? Why or why not?

ANSWERED PRAYERS

PRAY FOR CANADA

JOURNAL

DAY 11: NORTHWEST TERRITORIES

Journal

12
ALBERTA
Rocky Mountains, Canola, and Wheat

PRAY FOR CHRISTIANS IN ALBERTA:
- To put God first in their lives.
- To seek holiness.
- To grow in faith and boldness.

FUN FACTS:
- Alberta has the world's largest beaver dam, and it's visible from space.
- Alberta has approximately six hundred lakes.
- Alberta has the largest population of wild horses that roam free in all of Canada!
- The bear-proof garbage can was invented in Alberta.
- Banff National Park, Canada's first national park, was established in 1885.[14]

PRAY FOR CANADA

Scripture Reading: 1 Peter 4:7

When you hear the term *end-times*, what do you think of? Do you think you'll live to see the end-times, or do you think it will only happen hundreds of years from now?

It's interesting that Peter says that the end of all things is near. There seems to be a consistent theme throughout the New Testament letters to live with the expectation that the end is near.

This isn't something we see in our culture today. Very few people seem to talk about the end of all things. However, Peter connects this concept to being alert so we can pray.

Does the thought of Jesus returning make you want to pray more? Or does it make you want to hide?

What's In the News?
PERFORM AN ONLINE search and pray:

Find Two Churches to Pray for:

1.

2.

DAY 12: ALBERTA

Make some notes below about what you think the end-times will look like. Then search the Scriptures to see if what you think matches up with what Scripture tells us will happen. How can prayer help us to understand what the Bible tells us about the return of Jesus?

ANSWERED PRAYERS

PRAY FOR CANADA

JOURNAL

DAY 12: ALBERTA

JOURNAL

13
Yukon
Gold Rush Territory

Pray for Christians in the Yukon:
- To show kindness to their communities.
- To clearly hear the Lord's voice.
- To serve the Lord with all their heart, soul,
- Mind, and strength.

Fun Facts:
Did you know that the Yukon is home to:
- More moose than people.
- The second highest mountain in North America.
- The world's smallest desert.[15]

PRAY FOR CANADA

Scripture Reading: Proverbs 15:29

What a responsibility rests with Christians. Because the Lord is far from the wicked, but hears the prayers of the righteous, we need to pray for our country. That way, the Lord will hear us.

This kind of responsibility also grants us the privilege of praying for others who may not yet know Christ.

Think about the people you interact with on a relatively regular basis. Is there someone at the grocery store, gym, or gas station who might have questions about Jesus? How can we pray for them? How can we teach them about Jesus?

I have found that people often know that you have faith, or at least they know there is something different about you. They may want to have a conversation. It helps when we open doors that help others ask their questions in a nonjudgemental atmosphere. We need to remember that we all started somewhere and the Lord is capable of reaching anyone!

Check the News?

Is there anything in the Yukon news that needs prayer today? Record the needs below and pray:

Prayers for Yukon:

Find two churches to pray for. Send an email to each church to let them know you are praying for them today:

1.

2.

DAY 13: YUKON

The possibilities for prayer are endless. We can pray for our family and friends as well as people who live in countries all around the world. Make a list of three people you can commit to praying for over the next few weeks. See what the Lord will accomplish through your prayers.

ANSWERED PRAYERS

PRAY FOR CANADA

JOURNAL

DAY 13: YUKON

Journal

14

BRITISH COLUMBIA

The West Coast

DID YOU KNOW:
- About 90% of Canada's cougars live in B.C.
Canada has had two professional competitors in sumo, and both were from B.C.
- B.C. has the most living species of any Canadian province.
- The province has two time zones.[16]

SCRIPTURE READING: REVELATION 8:3–4

Have you ever thought about what happens to our prayers after we pray? Today's verses give us a glimpse of what happens in heaven. Imagine it: our words get poured out on an altar before the throne of God!

No matter how big or small your prayer is, it does go up before the Lord. No prayer is inadequate. Every single one is heard by the Lord.

In ancient times, the altar in the tabernacle and the first two temples in Israel played a central role in worship. Read Luke 1:8–17, in the New International Verision if possible. What was Zechariah doing in this passage, and what kind of a visitor did he receive? Where did the visitor stand? It's beautiful how the Lord gives us earthly pictures that mirror what happens before His throne in heaven.

PRAY FOR CANADA

As we come close to the end of this prayer journey, my prayer for you is that you will find strength in knowing that the Lord hears your prayers. They go up before His throne. Draw a picture of what you think this looks like.

Don't worry, we won't look at your picture!

SEARCH THE NEWS.
REcord two stories below and pray for what is happening in B.C..

FIND TWO CHURCHES TO PRAY FOR.
Email to see what their prayer requests are or check their church bulletins online:

1.

2.

DAY 14: BRITISH COLUMBIA

Answered Prayers

PRAY FOR CANADA

JOURNAL

DAY 14: BRITISH COLUMBIA

JOURNAL

15
Wrap Up

Write a final prayer below.

PRAY FOR CANADA

Dear Father,

We thank You for our country of Canada. We thank You for seeing what is happening around us. We ask that You accomplish something miraculous as we pray. Grow Your church here in this land, in all our provinces and territories. Let the fruit of the Spirit be evident in our lives. Give us boldness to share Your words, no matter how easy or difficult the circumstances may be around us. We thank You for having not given us a spirit of fear, but of power, love, and a sound mind (2 Timothy 1:7).

We repent for the sins we have committed personally and for decisions made by our leaders that may not line up with Your commands. We ask that You cleanse our hearts and heal our land as You heal us. We thank You for Your promise: *"If we confess our sins, he is faithful and just and will forgive us our sins and purify us from all unrighteousness"* (1 John 1:9, NIV). We ask that You would start a revival in our hearts individually, and that this would spread to those around us.

We pray that reverence for Your name would come to our land. Give us Your peace in the middle of every situation, both good and bad, so others will see You walking with us. Open our eyes to see where You are needed. Give us opportunities to share Your Gospel throughout our country.

As we see the time of Your return get nearer, prepare our hearts to go home to be with You. We thank You for all You have done for us! In Jesus's name, amen.

DAY 15: WRAP UP

Action Page

During this time of prayer, did you feel the Lord prompting you to do something specific? If so, please make some notes below about what He has prompted you to do and how you plan to accomplish it. If you did not feel a prompting but would like to know what the Lord would have you do, pray that He will show you what you need to do! Then start reading through the Scriptures so He can speak to you.

If you openly declare that Jesus is Lord and believe in your heart that God raised him from the dead, you will be saved. For it is by believing in your heart that you are made right with God, and it is by openly declaring your faith that you are saved.
(Romans 10:9-10, NLT)

Endnotes

1 "Island Economy," *Government of Prince Edward Island*. Date of access: November 13, 2024 (https://www.princeedwardisland.ca/en/information/executive-council-office/island-economy).

2 "Facts About Prince Edward Island," *Trip Shepherd*. April 10, 2023 (https://www.tripshepherd.com/blog/facts-about-prince-edward-island).

3 "History," *Bluenose II*. Date of access: November 21, 2024 (https://bluenose.novascotia.ca/history).

4 "NB Facts," *My New Brunswick*. Date of access: April 15, 2024 (https://mynewbrunswick.ca/nb-facts).

5 "Learn About the Province," *Find Newfoundland and Labrador*. April 15, 2024 (https://www.findnewfoundlandlabrador.com/).

6 "Fun Facts About Newfoundland and Labrador," *We Explore Canada*. March 6, 2024 (https://weexplorecanada.com/fun-facts-newfoundland-labrador).

7 Joe Lofaro, "Bill 21: Five Things About the Province's Contentious Secularism Law," *CTV News*. February 29, 2024 (https://montreal.ctvnews.ca/bill-21-five-things-about-the-province-s-contentious-secularism-law-1.6789575).

8 "America Demografia," *US Canada Info*. Date of Access: March 30, 2024 (https://uscanadainfo.com/religion-in-quebec).

9 "Fun Facts About Ontario," *Ultimate Ontario*. Date of access: November 13, 2024 (https://ultimateontario.com/fun-facts-about-ontario).

10 "Manitoba Premier Wants Daily Legislative Prayer to Be More Inclusive," *CBC*. April 11, 2024 (https://www.cbc.ca/news/canada/manitoba/prayer-legislature-question-period-refresh-1.7170772).

11 "13 Facts You Didn't Know About Nunavut," *Destination Nunavut*. Date of access: April 30, 2024 (https://destinationnunavut.ca/discover/13-facts-you-didnt-know-about-nunavut).

12 "Saskatchewan Facts," *Tourism Saskatchewan*. Date of access: May 1, 2024 (https://www.tourismsaskatchewan.com/about-saskatchewan/saskatchewan-facts).

13 "Living in the NWT," *Government of the Northwest Territories*. Date of access: May 1, 2024 (https://www.ece.gov.nt.ca/en/services/prospective-teacher-information/living-nwt).

14 "Banff National Park," *Town of Banff*. Date of access: November 21, 2024 (https://banff.ca/523/Banff-National-Park).

15 "8 Things You Didn't Know About Living in the Yukon," *Normandy Living*. Date of access: July 17, 2024 (https://www.normandyliving.com/blog/8-things-you-didnt-know-about-living-in-the-yukon).

16 "Cats, Culture, and Columbia: Fun Facts About B.C.," *You & Me BC*. Date of access: July 17, 2024 (https://www.youandmebc.ca/post/bc-facts).

www.ingramcontent.com/pod-product-compliance
Lightning Source LLC
Chambersburg PA
CBHW040253170426
43191CB00019B/2400